Exploring Careers

Jobs in Agribusiness

Exploring Careers

Jobs in Agribusiness

by Robert J. Houlehen

ILLUSTRATED WITH PHOTOGRAPHS

CONSULTANTS

Donald G. Schwarz, Dean
Agribusiness Division
Milwaukee Area Technical College
Milwaukee, Wisconsin

Carl M. Tausig, Ed.D., Research Specialist
Enrichment of Teacher and Counselor Competencies in
  Career Education
Center for Educational Studies
Eastern Illinois University
Charleston, Illinois

Lothrop, Lee & Shepard Company
NEW YORK

Also by Robert J. Houlehen

JOBS IN MANUFACTURING

1   2   3   4   5   78   77   76   75   74

Library of Congress Cataloging in Publication Data

Houlehen, Robert J
  Jobs in agribusiness.

  (Exploring careers)
  SUMMARY: Introduces the wide variety of career possibilities in the agricultural industries and services, such as meat inspector, landscape architect, ranch foreman, and forestry aide.
  1. Agricultural industries—Vocational guidance—Juvenile literature. [1. Agricultural industries—Vocational guidance]   I. Schwarz, Donald G., joint author.   II. Tausig, Carl M., joint author.   III. Title.
HD9000.5.H68   630′203   73-17714
ISBN 0-688-75005-2

Exploring Careers

Contents

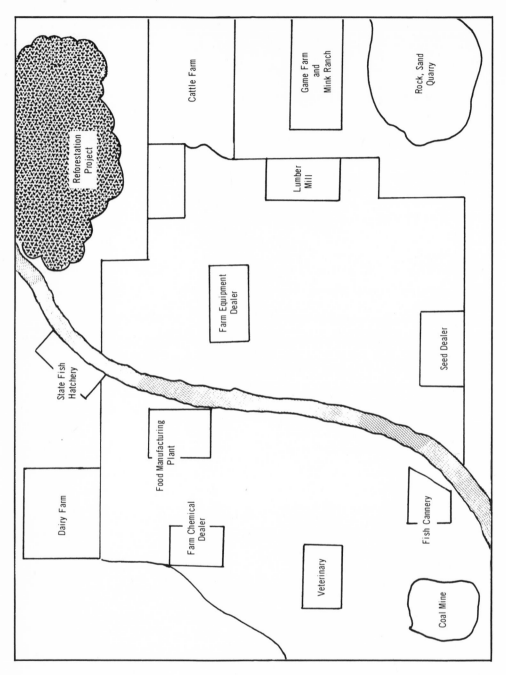

Many communities in North America center around agribusiness, just like the one drawn above.

Let's Have Some Definitions

Agribusiness is also called the food and fibers industry.

There are three important divisions in agribusiness. *Agriculture* is the growing of crops and raising of livestock. We also call agriculture "farming." There are some very special kinds of farming, such as raising trees and flowers.

Agricultural industry includes processing and manufacturing of food and fiber products. It includes getting foods and products to the people who use them. Finally, it includes the manufacture of machinery and other tools used in agriculture and agricultural industry.

Agricultural services refers to all kinds of aid given to people in agriculture and in the agricultural industry. Some of this help is also given to consumers by the government. A meat inspector for example, provides all of us with an agricultural service.

Everything Starts with the Land

The land and the water all around us provide our natural resources.

The land and the water give us our food. They give us the minerals to make useful articles. The trees provide raw materials and shelter our wildlife. In fact, we couldn't live without farming, forestry, fishing, and mining.

Production and sale of farm products, farm machinery, and food is the nation's biggest business. Everybody in our country is involved in it. Some of us are producers. All of us are users. One out of every five jobs is in the food industry. And what do we spend every year for things to eat? More than 100 billion dollars. About four and one-half million of us live and work on farms. Other millions of us make and sell equipment for farmers. Or we help them enrich their soil, kill bugs, and keep their livestock healthy. And even more millions of us work with the products of mines and oceans. Finally, thousands of Americans find rewarding careers in protecting and improving the land.

You may already have a career in agribusiness. If you are a teenager, you may be a packer in a store. If you live in a small town, you may help in a farm chemical store or tractor store. If you live on a farm, you may help to feed

These school students from Oregon are taking part in a large tree seed project. They are helping to produce seedlings for reforestation.

poultry and animals, milk cows, or work with machines in the fields. Even if you live in the city, you may be involved with our natural resources. You may have enjoyed days in the country, planting trees in a forest or park. You may have helped to clean a river.

Agribusiness has interesting jobs for people wherever they live. Many careers involve the forests, mines, and quarries. The oceans are becoming farms and mines of a very special type. They have exciting career areas of their own. And everywhere there are careers in the marketing, manu-

facturing, and distributing of products for mining, petroleum production, and lumbering.

Education and training for agribusiness jobs become
more available every year. Many schools can help prepare
people for such fields as:

Production agriculture (actual farming)

Services to agriculture and other natural resources fields

Manufacturing for agriculture and natural resources
fields

Conservation of resources

Forestry

Ocean sciences

Distribution of food products and other products

Recreation

Gardening and grounds maintenance

Government service for agribusiness and natural resources

Scientific research

Teaching in all these fields

Schools in farming states train in production farming.
Big city schools offer courses in gardening and florist skills.
Cattle area schools provide courses related to animals.
Where people work in the forests, there is training in fores-
try and wildlife conservation. Many colleges, for example,
specialize in agriculture, or mining, or ocean sciences.

Production Farming—
Grains and Corn

Production farming is raising food and fiber on a large scale. Even a *farmer* with ten acres is a production farmer if he sells what he grows.

Farmers have gone from subsistence farming to farming as a business. Subsistence farming means farming to feed one's family.

A *subsistence farmer* makes almost all of his tools. A *production farmer* buys almost everything. A subsistence farmer saves some of his crop for seeds. A production farmer buys seed. A subsistence farmer doctors his own animals. A production cattle raiser calls in a veterinary doctor.

No matter how big they are, production farms often are specialized. The owners raise only a few things. There are:

Corn and grain farms

Vegetable farms

General cattle ranches

Cattle feeder farms

Dairy farms

Poultry farms

Cotton, tobacco, and peanut farms

Recreation farms

Fur farms

Fruit orchards

14

Working the soil of a production crop farm goes on most of the year.
Machines are used for much of the work. Farmers are usually skilled in
keeping their machines in top condition.   *Darryl Priess*

There are two kinds of production farms: family farms and big business farms. The big business farms provide the greatest number of career possibilities. Located almost everywhere, most big business farms raise field crops. Chiefly, they are corn, grain, or vegetable farms.

No matter the size of a farm, there are employees to help make it go. Some are fairly unskilled. They may learn their work as they go along. General *farmhands* start by doing simple work. They load wagons, paint, do simple repair. As they progress, they run equipment and help with the buying and selling. If they wish, they learn enough to work their own farms. Or they may become good at mechanical work, and are hired by machinery firms.

FAMILY FARMS

Let's look at a family field crop farm.

The owner is probably the chief worker. He plans for his crops and prepares his soil and plants. He harvests and arranges to sell what he has produced. He does much of the repair work on his buildings and machines. Between times, he is a good citizen in his community. He may hold public office.

Who helps the family farmer? His wife and children do much of the work. Many family farmers hire some full-time or part-time workers. These people run farm machines such as tractors. They repair buildings and fences, clean barns, package crops, and drive trucks.

Family farmers do not have a chance for "promotion"

Hired hands, such as the man on the right, may be members of a farmer's family or workers who live nearby. Some hands may have farmlands of their own.

on the farm. Instead they may buy or rent more land. Or they may go into other businesses, such as selling and repairing farm machinery.

Young people on farms often buy or rent land for themselves. They become farm operators like their parents. Many find other careers in agribusiness. They become mechanics or salespeople for farm equipment stores. They drive trucks for milk companies. They become airplane pilots who dust crops with bug-killer powder. They become forest rangers or sawmill workers.

Young farm people often become *agricultural engineers*. Then they work for state governments, machinery makers, food processing companies. They may become *mechanical engineers* who design farm machinery.

BIG BUSINESS FARMS

There are more opportunities in big business field crop farms. These farms may be owned by a large firm or by a group of local farmers who form a company. They may even be owned by an individual farmer.

Big farms offer a range of careers. *Managers* plan for crops (or animals), guide sales work, hire people, train workers, direct repair work. Under them are specialized workers. A *field manager* directs planting and harvesting. A *sales manager* finds markets for the products and helps plan future production. A *chief mechanic* keeps all the equipment running. If many animals are involved, a full-time *veterinarian* or animal doctor may be employed. A

18

Farmers never stop learning. These grain farmers are getting new ideas about harvesting at a short course run by a machinery dealer.

Robert J. Houlehen

transportation manager runs a truck fleet. There may even be a *storekeeper* or toolroom clerk who gives tools to workers. A *personnel* or *employment manager* hires and trains workers and keeps employment records.

Service workers are everywhere on a big business farm. As in many businesses, they are specialized and often belong to labor unions. Some operate farm machinery as their chief jobs. Some do mechanical or electrical repair work. Others are carpenters or painters.

Some big business farms also may run food processing plants such as canneries. They may also have food warehouses. Employees run processing machinery or lift trucks and conveyors. Some pack food products.

More and more big and small full-time production farmers are well educated for their work. Many owners are college graduates. They have had courses in agricultural economics, practical mechanics, and chemistry. On big farms, many of the managers and specialists also are college-trained. Many of the service employees are well prepared by their high schools and vocational schools.

Big business farm managers often move into bigger jobs in their companies. Production and service workers often move into supervisory jobs or into larger firms. Some go into agricultural services businesses.

You don't have to live on a farm to be a farmer. Thousands of working farmers live in villages and cities. They may even hold other jobs. They usually have high school educations. Many have technical school certificates or college degrees.

Education at an agricultural college can open many interesting doors for men and women.   *The University of Tennessee*

Men and women in colleges seem to want farm careers more than ever. Crop farming may appeal to them because the work is seasonal. There is time for other things. In recent years the flow of young people leaving farms for city work has been reversed a little. People are turning back to outdoor living and healthy work.

People on farms are discovering they can have several careers at once. They manage or own tourist camps, lakes for fishermen, produce stores, antique shops. They can make furniture, create rugs and quilts, operate food pro-

21

cessing plants. They can generate electricity and pump water. They can run a lumber mill and own a weekly paper.

They can also add specialized agriculture or ranching to their operations. In this way, they help keep people at work. When one type of production is closed for the season, another may be going strong. Animals and birds, for example, require all year-round care. In fact, many field crop farms also have various kinds of special agriculture and ranching as part of their operations.

The greenhouse operator is a horticulturist who doesn't have to run his business in the country. *Milwaukee Area Technical College*

JOBS IN PRODUCTION FARMING

Job	Education	Training	Duties	Opportunities
Crop specialty farmhand	High school, skill courses	On-the-job	Perform wide variety of work for specific crops	Become manager or foreman, work for dealer or manufacturer, buy own farm
Equipment operator	High school	On-the-job, dealer courses	Drive machines for plowing, cultivating, planting, fertilizing, weed killing	Become manager or foreman, work for dealer or manufacturer
Farmer, full-time	High school, agricultural college, vocational courses	On-the-job, dealer course	Plan for crops machinery, sale of product	Own more land, add related business to farm work
Farmer, part-time	High school	On-the-job, reading, any course available	Same	May have another career as well
Farmhand, general	Most possible	On-the-job	Any work not needing special skills	Take vocational agriculture courses, become specialized, learn mechanics

Job	Education	Training	Duties	Opportunities
Farm manager	High school, often agricultural college	On-the-job, special courses	Manage for the owners—planning, maintenance, hiring, training, field work	Become owner, go into machinery or food business
Field driver (trucks)	High school	On-the-job, truck dealer courses	Drive trucks used in harvest, hauling planter supply, fertilizer supply	Become equipment operator, special crop farmhand, work for dealer, become dealer
Mechanic	High school, technical school	Manufacturer or dealer courses	Repair machines, prevent breakdowns by regular care	Work for dealer as parts-service mechanic or manager, work for manufacturer as service representative

24

Specialized Crops from Flowers to Onions

When we think of production farming, we may imagine thousands of acres of golden wheat. Or we may think of endless rows of corn. These huge crops can be harvested by big machines. They are shipped to big storage centers and sold anywhere in the world.

But a great many of the production farms are smaller. Their crops are sold nearby and may be used right away. Many vegetable farms sell to canning plants only miles away. Some vegetable farms also have their own canning factories. Many kinds of fruit are sold for local use. Some are rushed to distant markets for sale fresh during the winter. Flowers are hurried in refrigerator cars or on planes to other communities.

Raising these products of the soil—vegetables, fruits, flowers, nuts, and ornamental plants—is a special part of agriculture called horticulture. You can be a *horticulturalist* and live and work in a city. You can receive all your training and education in a city. Of course, you can learn all you need to know in many smaller places as well.

Horticulture has its own kinds of producers, suppliers, and manufacturers. There are educators and researchers and helpful government agencies in this field, too.

Jobs in Agribusiness

All the typical careers found in corn-grain farming are found in fruits and vegetables. There are the owners and their families who may do much of this seasonal work. If their properties are large or if they have other businesses, they may hire full-time or part-time employees.

Managers, foremen and special *crop workers* all have experience and training for their work. General workers may start with only little experience.

Fruit orchard workers must understand planting and cultivating of trees. They also know how to spray, prune, pick, and harvest. In big orchards, workers may be hired for specific work, such as pruning or spraying. Often or-

Mushroom farmers raise their crops in the dark—even in old mines and caves. This underground equipment operator is moving the huge dirt-filled boxes in which mushrooms are growing. *Butler County Mushroom Farms*

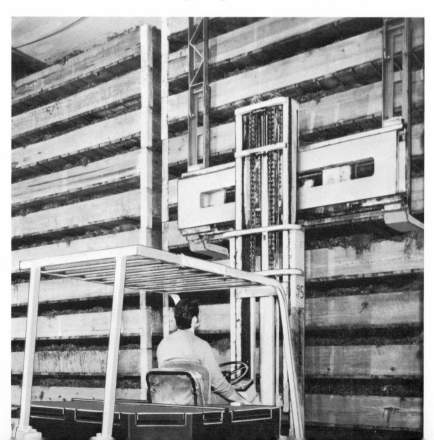

chard owners and employees have taken special courses in high school. Or they have taken courses given by suppliers of equipment, seeds, and chemicals. Orchards have their own equipment, such as fruit pickers. The workers must be trained to run and maintain them.

All this is true for people working with vegetables. In addition, these workers must understand irrigation of crops that need much water. They must be able to handle pumps and the engines that drive them.

These jobs are much like those of corn and grain production farming. In fact, many farmers raise corn in one area, apples in another, and beets in a third.

A grower—a name used when orchards, greenhouses, or gardens are involved—needs land, just like a field crop farmer. He may also need special buildings that are lighted, heated, ventilated, and provided with water.

VEGETABLE GROWER

A vegetable grower is also called a *truck farmer*. He may have a small farm and produce for a few regular customers. Or he may have a large operation and sell his goods to grocery chains or through fruit and vegetable merchants. These merchants, or brokers, find markets for the grower.

Truck farmers usually have full-time and part-time workers. They hire many seasonal workers to plant, cultivate, spray, irrigate, pick, clean, and pack the crops. Regular workers include *foremen of field operations, greenhouse foremen, equipment operators* and specialty farmhands.

27

The regular workers start seeds in greenhouses or hotbeds. They also do the endless repair and maintenance of buildings and equipment.

FRUIT GROWERS

Fruit growers may also have other farming operations. Sometimes they sell to one customer. A winery, for example, buys cherries. Sometimes growers sell to produce canners or stores.

A great portion of a fruit grower's work is planning and supervising employees and equipment. Some crops are started from seed every year. Some are raised on perennial plants, such as apple trees. All these crops require part-time helpers. There are a few helpers during early days and a great many at picking time. Because of fruit's delicacy, time and equipment are spent weeding and killing insects. Frost can hurt crops. So can almost any excess in weather. Part-time help can be quite skillful. They may move from crop to crop or live in the community and have winter jobs.

As the work of raising fruits and vegetables becomes more complicated so does the equipment. Additional education and training are needed. Some growers are agricultural college graduates. Some learn on the job and through special courses. Others learn through vocational agricultural training in high school. But they do not work alone, nor do corn and grain farmers. Many government agencies and private services help them solve disease problems, plan crops, and improve output.

These equipment operators prepare loaded boxes of apples for movement into cold storage. *Van's Industrial Equipment, Inc.*

Jobs in Agribusiness

FLOWER GROWERS

Flower growers may run their colorful businesses right in a city neighborhood. Or they might be in small towns or in the farmlands between communities.

As you drive along a country road, a twinkle of reflected sunshine catches your eye. There are rows of greenhouses in the distance. Great splashes of color in the fields mean you are passing a flower raiser's farm. He also may have acres of young trees and shrubs. This will be transplanted

The crop specialists in this tree and shrub nursery are caring for new pine trees. *Milwaukee County Park Commission*

to homes, parks, golf courses, and cemeteries. There may be other acres of rich green grass ready to be cut up into rolls of turf.

The owner and his workers are well trained in growing and selling all these products. What are their jobs? *Field hands* plant, cultivate, water, and protect the young trees and shrubs. Usually they have machinery to help them. Inside workers are called *nursery* or *greenhouse workers.* They do much of their work with small, simple tools.

The whole operation may have a *nursery manager.* He or she is possibly college-trained in agriculture and business administration. *Shipping clerks* arrange for hauling or mailing of the living products. *Truck drivers* are needed, particularly at busy seasons. The office has accountants, clerks for typing and filing, and sometimes a specialist in purchasing. Often nursery hands will transplant trees and shrubs for a customer.

There may be garden centers right in your community. These sell plants, flowers, tools, and supplies. They also provide service to people with lawns, trees, shrubs, and flowers. There may be *landscape architects,* who plan large lawns and gardens for big homes, office buildings, parks and golf courses, schools, and apartment buildings. And there may be a lawn and garden service company. Employees of this company will handle lawn, tree, and shrub care for anybody who needs the service.

You don't have to live on a farm or ranch to be involved with agribusiness. But you do need to live "out in the coun-

This landscape architect and his young helpers are discussing tree shapes.
Milwaukee Area Technical College

try" to be involved with another part of this industry: raising and selling birds and animals and their products. That's another chapter.

JOBS IN HORTICULTURE

Job	Education	Training	Duties	Opportunities
Architect, land-scape	College	Courses after college, manufacturers' schools	Plan use of land, flowers, trees, grass for homes, schools, offices, factories, parks etc. Guide actual work	Run own business, form contracting company, run nurseries, stores. Teach.
Contractor, land-scape	High school, technical courses	Manufacturers' courses, on-the-job	Perform work planned by architect, highway engineers, home owner, park superintendent. Move earth, plant major trees, move rocks, gravel, lay sod	Expand business, open stores, become grower
Crop specialist, horticulture	High school, technical courses	Manufacturers' courses, on-the-job	Handle technical work of preparation, planting, spraying, pruning	Become grower, open store, become manufacturers' salesperson
Designer, land-scape	High school, technical courses	On-the-job, manufacturers' and growers' courses	Make plans for architect, garden center, contractor	Study architecture, become grower or contractor
Designer, floral	High school, technical courses	On-the-job, technical programs by schools, associations	Arrange flowers for use	Become florist, grower, landscape designer

33

Job	Education	Training	Duties	Opportunities
Equipment operator	High school	On-the-job	Run machines used by growers	Become mechanic, grower, foreman; become manufacturers' mechanic or salesperson
Florist, retail	High school, technical school, sometimes agricultural college	Special school courses, manufacturers' courses	Run store selling to public	Expand business, become grower, operate garden center
Florist salesperson	High school	On-the-job, technical courses	Help public buy, help with packaging, delivery	Study to be floral designer, florist, grower, store manager
Fruit farmer	High school, technical school or agricultural college	Graduate courses, manufacturers' courses	Operate orchard or farm. Plan, plant, protect, harvest. Hire and train, manage finances	Expand property, add crops, open stores, run a warehouse, become equipment dealer
Garden center manager	High school, technical courses, business courses	On-the-job, manufacturers' courses	Plan and conduct operations of the store, growing areas, and the machinery repair shop. Hire and train employees	Open own center, become a landscape contractor, become salesperson for manufacturer, become park superintendent, become golf course superintendent

Garden center mechanic	High school, technical school	Repair customers' power and manual tools	Become garden center manager, become equipment dealer, open garden center
Garden center salesperson	High school, technical courses	Help customers with purchases, make recommendations, solve problems, demonstrate	Become garden center manager, open own center, or train for almost any other horticultural career
Gardener	High school, technical courses	Care for flowers, shrubs, trees and grass of estate, park, office building, college etc.	Study for work as golf course superintendent and similar jobs, open garden center, become landscape contractor
Golf course superintendent	College, technical courses	Plan and operate maintenance program, buy and maintain vehicle fleet, hire and train employees	Become equipment dealer, open a garden center, become grower, become manufacturers' salesperson
Greenhouse manager	High school, technical school	On-the-job, special courses, business courses	Run greenhouse operations for owner. May be owner
Greenhouse manager	High school, technical school	Run greenhouse operations for owner. May be owner	Become owner, expand duties, become grower of other crops, become suppliers' salesperson

Job	Education	Training	Duties	Opportunities
Greenskeeper	High school	On-the-job	Maintain grass, sand traps, shrubs, trees, flowers on golf course	Study, train for superintendent's post, can learn almost anything in horticulture
Ground maintenance employee	High school	On-the-job, technical courses	Perform wide range of outdoor duties on estates, cemeteries, parks etc. Also do snow removal, equipment repair, furniture repair	Study for almost any post in horticulture
Park superintendent (also cemetery)	High school, technical courses	On-the-job, manufacturers' courses	Plan and operate outdoor programs, hire and train employees, maintain and buy equipment, keep furniture and other property in good order	Go into own horticulture business, become manufacturer or manufacturers' salesperson
Tree pruner	High school, technical courses		Do actual tree pruning, help surgeon	Study for post as surgeon, can work into almost any horticulture career
Tree surgeon	High school, technical courses	Special courses, manufacturers' courses	Prune and repair trees	Go into own business anywhere in horticulture

Production Farming with Poultry and Livestock

There was a time when farmers let their chickens, cows, and ducks scratch for food in the farmyard or meadow. Today, raising livestock and poultry is a specialty. Their growth and health is never left to chance.

Today's specialists raise hens that lay a great many eggs. They find ways to make dairy cows produce a lot of milk. Their pigs have leaner meat and their turkeys have meatier chests.

Behind each pork chop and each egg may be a team of experts. They gather new information about birds and animals and work closely with the specialists.

As a result of this scientific approach, many new careers have appeared.

Today you can be a specialist in:

Raising cattle for meat and hides

Raising sheep for wool and meat

Raising cows for dairy products and, to some extent, meat

Raising chickens for meat and eggs

Raising turkeys, geese, and ducks for meat

Raising goats for dairy products

A ranch hand must lift and shift a good deal of feed by hand.

Frank Lassiter

Some of the new careers include breeding birds or animals to be sold to ranchers, poultry farmers, or dairy farmers. Another job may be feeding young cattle, bought from ranchers, until they are ready to sell for food.

38

Some of these farming operations have many kinds of jobs connected with them, some only a few.

Cattle ranching is a year-round operation. Jobs there are year-round, too. There are *livestock farmhands* who may be cowboys or who may work around the ranch. Because as much ranching is done from trucks as from horses, there may be a farm mechanic. If many employees live on the ranch, there may be a cook.

Very large ranches have some special workers, too. General farmhands may raise feed crops needed by the animals. These farmhands plant, cultivate, weed, and harvest. They operate machines to speed up their work. There may also be a carpenter to do the endless repair of buildings.

Some ranches have large horse herds, so blacksmiths are on the payroll. So are *stablemen,* who care for the horses and their barns. A big ranch may have a *cattle dehorner* who cuts down sharp horns. However, the dehorner and the blacksmith very well might be in business for themselves in nearby towns.

Running a dairy farm is a year-round job for the *dairyman* and his family. He doesn't always need as much range or grassland for feeding as does a rancher. *Dairy farmhands* may do some of their feeding from special wagons taken to the pastures. Other feeding, particularly in cold weather, is done indoors. A dairy farm needs a great deal of machinery for milking cows and preparing milk for delivery to the dairies. The dairy farmer may take care of this machinery himself. If he has a big farm, there may be a mechanic for this work.

Neatness is important where food is involved. This dairy farmer doesn't go near his cattle in dirty clothes.   *The Farmer*

Chicken raising is somewhat different from dairying or ranching. This is because chicken farming is highly automated. Big chicken farms do not let their birds run loose. The poultry is kept in long houses. Eggs are removed on moving belts and food is often provided by machinery. Chickens grow quickly. They are killed and prepared for sale right on the chicken farm.

This special way of raising chickens for meat and eggs has created some new jobs.

Often chicken farms are owned by organizations called cooperatives. The farmers provide many services for themselves through this central organization. Other chicken farms may be owned by companies. Each chicken farm owned by a company has a *manager,* who hires poultry farmhands and some specialists in poultry raising. A very important specialist is a *chick sexer.* He or she determines the sex of each new chick. Roosters are usually raised for meat. Hens are usually raised for eggs.

What about farmers who raise turkeys, geese, or ducks? These large birds are raised for meat. Some are sold regularly all year round, some are sold at holiday times. Otherwise, operations on these farms are similar to those on chicken farms. General farmhands take care of the birds. Special service may come from experts, who are self-employed or who are government employees.

Some specialists breed birds. All over the country there are hatcheries. Eggs laid by the female birds are hatched in warm boxes. The chicks are later sold to farmers, who will either raise them as egg-layers or for meat.

41

Production Farming with Poultry and Livestock

One of the new jobs is *eggroom foreman*. He or she examines eggs bought from poultry farmers or eggs laid by the hatchery's own flock. He also has workers whom he trains to catch eggs that will not produce suitable chicks. Hatchery hands also load the incubators, remove hatched chicks and clean the incubators. Very likely, a maintenance worker keeps the machinery operating.

Animal breeding is a more complicated operation. Breeders produce animals that will make good meat or good wool. Animal breeding farms have all the typical animal farm jobs. In addition, there may be a full-time veterinary doctor or at least a *paravet,* trained and experienced for animal care. Even the farm hands are selected and trained for their interest in animals.

No description of animal farms would be complete without mention of fur farms. Driving through the countryside, you may see rows of very small buildings, surrounded by fences. You may be looking at a mink, fox, or rabbit ranch. Usually the owner and a helper or two do all the work of breeding, feeding, killing, and skinning the animals. Expert help on breeding or feeding sometimes comes from experienced veterinarians or from associations of fur animal raisers.

Thinking of going into some sort of animal raising? "It's

Raising poultry is a year-round and day-long job. Specialized workers bring the chicks to maturity through a scientific program.

Washington Farmer and Stockman

The veterinarian keeps records on the health of his client's cattle, birds, or other animals.   *Frank Lassiter*

demanding work," an old-timer explained. "The animals can't do much for themselves."

Yet there is much help for people in agriculture, particularly from the "input" industries that make up agribusiness.

JOBS IN ANIMAL FARMING

Job	Education	Training	Duties	Opportunities
Animal groom	High school, technical courses	On-the-job, special courses	Clean animals, prepare for shows and special events	Train for post as foreman or paravet, start supply business, buy own farm
Breeder	High school, agricultural college	Graduate courses, special courses	Operate farm for producing carefully selected young animals, birds. Keep animal records, plan feeding, buy new breeding stock. Sell animals	Expand business.
Cattle dehorner	High school, technical courses	On-the-job, manufacturers' courses	Use mechanical, chemical means to remove or prevent horn growth	Study, train for any field in cattle raising
Cattleman	High school, technical courses, agricultural college	On-the-job, special courses, manufacturers' courses; association courses; suppliers' courses	Plan, operate cattle ranch, hire, train personnel, sell cattle, repair buildings, machines, plan crops	Expand business, get into related business, such as vacation ranch
Chick sexer	High school, technical courses	On-the-job	Determine sex of young chicks	Become manager, open own hatchery, work for feed store

Job	Education	Training	Duties	Opportunities
Dairy farmhand	High school, technical courses	Same as above	Assist owner in all dairy work	Become owner, sell for supplier, open dealership for feed, machinery
Dairy herdsman	High school, agricultural college	On-the-job, special courses, suppliers' courses, government courses	Plan and operate dairy farm, buy and sell cattle, hire and train employees, keep records	Expand farm, enter related businesses
Egg room foreman	High school, technical courses	On-the-job, association courses, government courses	Conduct examination of eggs, eliminate those unfit for hatching	Become hatchery manager, owner, become supplier salesperson or supplier of feed and equipment
Feed lot operator	High school, technical courses, agricultural college	On-the-job, suppliers' courses, government courses	Operate cattle feeder farm, prepare young cattle for sale	Expand business, open related business, become feed, equipment dealer
Fur rancher	High school, technical courses, game management courses	Association courses, suppliers' courses	Operate fur ranch, care for animals, arrange for breeding, hire and train workers, sell skins and young	Enter fur manufacturing, add other farming projects, become dealer, expand

Hatchery manager	High school, technical courses, perhaps some agricultural college	On-the-job, suppliers' and manufacturers' courses	Operate hatchery, sell chicks, hire and train employees	Become poultry farmer, enter other production business, become feed or equipment dealer
Poultry farmer	High school, technical courses, agricultural college	Association courses, government courses, suppliers' courses	Plan and direct all farm operations, repair and buy equipment, hire and train employees, sell products	Expand business, add related businesses, become dealer
Ranch foreman	High school, technical courses	Same as above	Operate specific parts of ranch operations	Own property, become ranch manager, become dealer for equipment, supplies
Sheep or pig farmer	High school, technical courses, agricultural college	Special courses, government courses, suppliers' and manufacturers' courses	Plan and direct all farm operations, hire and train employees, maintain equipment, sell products	Expand business, add related businesses, become dealer

Industry and Service in Agribusiness

If you were to drive through a small town in a farm area, you'd find agribusiness everywhere. There are stores selling machinery, seeds, and chemicals. There are banks, insurance firms, technical associations, and government offices. You would see the offices of veterinary doctors, conservation experts, and many others. There might be an agricultural college, a technical school, or a high school with agricultural courses.

You would be in an agribusiness town. This is a community in which almost everybody does something for the farmers and ranchers for miles around. Some residents may be farmers, too. This concern with agriculture isn't unusual. About forty percent of all workers in the United States are employed in agribusiness.

You can easily sort out people's work in an agribusiness town. Much of it involves agricultural services. There are:

1. General services, such as financial help, machinery and repair, electricity and gas, construction, and building materials.
2. Services for crop raisers, including technical assistance from government and associations, seeds and chemicals, planting and harvesting service.

An excellent career can be built around doing just one job—but for many farmers on many farms. This sign tells the world that the truck owner harvests field crops and takes them to the grain buyers' warehouses.

Robert J. Houlehen

3. Services for animal and bird raisers, including technical assistance from government and associations, and veterinary service.

First, let's look into general services.

Machinery and supply dealers are everywhere. They sell and take care of planting-harvesting machines, trucks and cars, prefabricated buildings, silos for crop storage, fences, pumps for water, small generators for electricity.

Most dealers own their businesses, but they buy and re-sell products made by manufacturing firms. You might see a big sign on one dealer's building reading "John Deere Tractors." This dealer resells John Deere tractors and other Deere farm machines. Then you might notice another sign on his building reading, "Ford Trucks." He also sells trucks. And another sign reading, "XYZ Co. Pumps." He also sells pumps. A dealer buys and sells everything he knows the farmers and ranchers need for their work. However, he tries to specialize, because he can't be expert in everything. He also operates a repair shop for all these machines. He tries to have all the parts his customers need for repairs. Dealers usually have the same kinds of employees. In addition to the owner, there may be a *sales manager,* who finds customers. Several *salesclerks* may work for this manager. The *parts and service manager* handles the repair shop and may have mechanics working with him. If the firm is big enough, there may be an accountant, a file clerk, a secretary to handle correspondence.

Right next door to the dealer's big equipment-filled lot may be a farm store. In many ways it's like a department store, but its merchandise is special. It's for farming and ranching. There are fence posts and bug killers, lighting fixtures and spades. There are wheels for do-it-yourself carts, and fence wire. Very likely the store is a "cooperative." This means its customers—or many of them—own the store and share in the profits. There's a store manager,

This farm store manager is as expert with hardware as she is with fabrics, kitchen equipment, or furniture. Her big store sells everything. *The Farmer*

perhaps a woman with a strong farm background. She has several farm-trained clerks to help customers make selections and solve problems. Another employee may run the dock. He receives incoming merchandise and loads goods for delivery.

Turn around the corner and you'll find another service that everybody needs: the electric cooperative. This business buys electricity from big power generating companies. It delivers electricity over its wires to farms, homes, stores, factories, schools, and churches. This customer-owned cooperative has many employees.

Power linemen put up poles, string wire, install power-controling transformers. Or they may install equipment underground. They install meters and fix lines damaged in storms.

Interior decorators help plan kitchens using electricity.

Computer operators and *programmers* keep financial and power-use records on complex office machines.

Billing clerks keep track of customer bills and payments.

Home economists run classes in cooking with electrical equipment.

Electrical technicians help install electrical equipment.

A big sign on a store front announces the county *agricultural agent's* office. Almost every county in the country has an agent. He or she works for three employers: the

These power linemen work for a rural electrification cooperative.
Wisconsin REC News Magazine

Jobs in Agribusiness

U.S. Department of Agriculture; the county; and the state land-grant college. The agent coordinates, or brings together, all manner of services for agribusiness.

He teaches good farming methods and helps associations and clubs arrange training projects. He advises farmers on construction of ponds and buildings.

Several assistants, often young people, help the agent.

A good deal of the agricultural agent's work is educational. Here he starts a demonstration in home gardening. *Milwaukee County Agricultural Agent*

One may be a cattle and poultry specialist, another a planting-harvesting expert. Each agent's office is special. Agricultural communities aren't all alike.

Outside the local bank you may see two or three men in farm work clothes chatting with a man in town clothes. He's the bank's *agricultural officer*. His job is to help farmers and agribusiness people manage their money. Some of his work is education. He is a regular speaker at meetings. Some of his work is technical. He helps farmers borrow money for buying equipment, paying bills, expanding.

One of the agricultural specialists who works in a bank is the *farm real estate appraiser*. He determines what farm properties are worth. Like the agricultural officer, he's trained in his field and keeps up to date through government agencies and technical associations. Or the appraiser may be a self-employed real estate broker. He helps people sell or buy farm properties.

Off to the edge of town, you'll find a grain dealer's plant or elevator. Huge tubelike buildings are used to store grains until they can be sold to food processing companies. The storage part of the business is simple. Machinery does most of the work. The grain *elevator manager* has a few helpers who run the machinery. One of them is also a mechanic. A few clerks keep the records of products received from farmers and a buyer keeps in touch with farmers.

Right across the street is another branch of the corn and grain industry: the feed and seed store. There are many kinds of feeds, depending on the animals and birds being raised. The owner manages the store and warehouse. He is helped by several men who load trucks and make deliveries. A *feed specialist* prepares special mixes for customers. An accountant keeps the mountains of business records in order.

The golden kernels of dry grains are stored in buildings called elevators. Here, an elevator manager and his general helper look over grains that will be sold to companies that make food.

JOBS THAT SERVICE AGRIBUSINESS

Job	Education	Training	Duties	Opportunities
Animal technician	High school, technical school	Special courses, on-the-job	Prepare animals for treatment at veterinary hospital, care for sick animals, perform laboratory tests	Return to school and study veterinary medicine, become salesperson for medical supplies, become herdsman, rancher
Artificial inseminator, livestock	High school, agricultural college, advanced courses	Special courses, government courses, graduate work	Improve animal qualities through arranging best parents, raise breeding stock, collect sperm, inject animals with sperm, counsel ranchers, farmers	Teach, expand business, become rancher, farmer, become manufacturer
Bank agricultural officer	High school, business administration courses, vocational agriculture courses, business college	Technical courses, graduate work	Assist farmers in obtaining loans, counsel on using money	Move into higher positions, obtain appointment to government agencies
Building service owner	High school, technical courses	On-the-job, suppliers' courses	Build, repair and maintain agricultural buildings	Expand business, acquire new businesses
Computer operator	High school, technical school	Manufacturers' courses	Run computer for cooperative, government agency, school serving agriculture and agribusiness, train employees, educate users	Work for larger organization, become equipment salesperson for computer maker, set up a computer service business

Job	Education	Training	Duties	Opportunities
Cooperative manager	High school, business school	Government agency courses, extension courses	Conduct all operations of businesses owned by the customers, train employees, look for business opportunities	Expand the co-op, enter private business, enter government service, buy farm
County agent	High school, agricultural college	Graduate courses, government agency courses	Assist all manner of agricultural persons in solving problems, run short courses, publicize opportunities in agriculture	Become teacher, become dealer
Dealer, equipment and supplies	High school, technical school	Manufacturers' courses	Sell and service goods bought from manufacturer, train salespeople, do special work for customers	Expand business, acquire added businesses
Electrical installer	High school, technical school	Manufacturers' courses, on-the-job	Deliver and hook up electrical equipment	Become service manager, become dealer
Electrical linesman, co-op	High school, technical school	Manufacturers' courses, government courses, on-the-job	Put up electrical poles, string power lines	Become supervisor, study and train to become cooperative manager
Farm store manager	High school, business college	Extension courses, graduate courses	Plan and conduct all store and warehouse operations, train employees, keep records, bill and collect, advertise	Expand business; become dealer

Grain elevator manager	High school, technical school	Government courses, processors' courses	Operate buildings and equipment in which grain is stored, buy and sell grain, arrange rail, truck shipment, maintain equipment	Expand business, become dealer, advance to higher post
Home economist	High school, college	Graduate courses, manufacturers' courses	Assist families to plan nutrition, rooms, room arrangement, clothing, may work for school, co-op, dealer, manufacturer	Become teacher, become salesperson
Mechanic, dealer	High school, technical school	Manufacturers' courses, on-the-job	Service and repair machinery sold by dealer	Become service and parts manager, become dealer, become salesperson for equipment maker
Nutritionist, livestock	High school, agricultural college	Graduate courses, government agency courses, manufacturers' courses	Work for feed manufacturers, feed dealers, large farmers, plan food for animals, observe feeding effects, plan new feeds	Become teacher, become feed dealer, become manager for manufacturer

Occupation	Education	Training	Duties	Advancement
Parts salesperson	High school	On-the-job	Keep parts section of dealership in order, help buyers make selections, deliver	Become parts manager, train to become mechanic, become dealer
Real estate broker	High school, technical school	Government courses, real estate association courses	Help farmers and agribusiness firms sell properties, help find properties to buy	Expand business, become dealer, open related businesses
Seed store manager	High school, technical school	Manufacturers' courses, extension courses	Manage all store activities, help farmers plan crops and care during growing	Expand business, acquire new businesses, become seed grower
Service manager	High school, technical school	Manufacturers' courses, on-the-job	Conduct maintenance and repair operations for equipment dealer, train employees, train users	Become dealer, become field service manager for manufacturer
Teacher, vocational agriculture	High school, agricultural college	Graduate, government agency courses	Conduct courses for young people, conduct special advanced courses for adults, cooperate with county agent	Become college instructor, become county agent, become school principal
Veterinarian	High school, veterinary college	Manufacturers' courses, government agency courses, graduate courses	Provide medical service of all kinds for birds and animals	Become college instructor, become employee of state or federal food agencies, enter armed forces

Processing and Manufacturing are Important Parts of Agribusiness

You can be a busy worker in agribusiness, yet seldom see a production farm, a tree nursery, or a ranch. Hundreds of jobs can be done in factories, in offices, in cities.

Some jobs are in processing. This means turning products of the fields into food and cloth. Some jobs are in factories that make machinery and supplies for lumbering, farming, or commercial fishing. Many more jobs are in food and fiber warehouses. Finally, a great many jobs are in sales and service offices. Employees here seek customers, help them buy, and help them use their purchases successfully.

Suppose you work in a factory that makes machinery used by corn and grain farmers. All over the factory you'll find men and women operating tools that cut and drill metal. Others run welding equipment that fastens metal pieces together. Others assemble parts into complete machines. Everywhere men and women operate lift trucks, cranes, and small carts. Others run sweeping machines, paint walls, count parts, or help other workers.

Do they need to know much about farms, veterinary

Both men and women do assembly work in equipment factories. They are often trained in specific skills and they must understand plans and other instructions. *Allis-Chalmers Corp.*

doctors, equipment dealers, and county agents? Not at all!

It's in marketing, sales, and design engineering departments that manufacturing for farms, ranches, parks, and gardens becomes different from manufacturing for homes, schools, and shopping centers. Farm marketing specialists

62

are very likely from farms. Engineers who design tree cut-
ters know how to use these machines. Salespeople who
visit dealers or the actual machinery users know a lot about
crops, cattle breeding, and tree transplanting.

You would be startled by the difference between a food-
processing plant and a tractor plant. The food processing
plant does much of its work inside tanks and pipes. It's

Agricultural engineers may construct models as a guide to what a machine
or building might look like. *University of Wisconsin*

cleaner and quieter than a metals or wood products factory.

More than five million people in our country process vegetables, pack meat, bake bread, prepare beverages, and make ice cream. Most of the food we eat is processed. It is cleaned, cut, cooked, and packaged in factories.

Food processing factories can be huge. They might make thirty or forty different kinds of canned products, delivered by dozens of trailer trucks. Some might have only four or five employees, including the owner. While the big companies have more kinds of jobs, there are more little food processing companies. So, let's lift the lid on a large food processor to see as many jobs as we can.

"We started out small," explains the president. "We had a girl cutting up pickles. Another ran the cooker. I did the bottling and my wife pasted on the labels. My two sons packed the pickles into cases and I drove the delivery truck."

Then he explains that among his hundreds of employees he now has some specialists:

Food technologists—They develop new foods and ways to prepare them.

Quality inspectors—They make sure products are acceptable to users.

Food graders—They determine the quality of raw foods.

This production worker operates a mixer in a food plant. His machine heats, cools, mixes, adds air, and removes air. *Food Processing Magazine*

Processing equipment engineers—They plan for special processing machinery.

Chemists—They help make food easy to keep and good to eat.

Laboratory technicians—They help chemists and food technologists.

Process supervisors—They direct operations in the "kitchen."

Cold storage managers—They run cold warehouses.

Sanitary engineers—They keep things clean.

Food buyers—They buy the raw materials for the factory.

Equipment service and maintenance supervisors—They keep machinery running.

Consumer affairs consultants—They help stores and consumers use the food products.

All of these workers need some training in technical or vocational schools or in colleges.

An important link between the food processing business and you is wholesale food distribution. The big trucks that bring canned foods, meats, and vegetables to your local grocery may come from food wholesalers.

Wholesalers buy foods from manufacturers and growers. The wholesaler employs salespeople to find stores and sell foods to it.

These computer room technicians can follow every food preparation job by watching the television sets and the lighted "maps" of the plant.

Food Processing Magazine

This consumer affairs consultant shows buyers how to use her company's products. *The Farmer Magazine*

JOBS IN PROCESSING & MANUFACTURING

Job	Education	Training	Duties	Opportunities
Agricultural engineer	High school, engineering college or agricultural college	Manufacturers' courses, technical association	Develop machinery and methods to help and improve farming, processing, soil use, water use	Become manager of departments, form own company, teach, obtain government agency jobs
Design engineer	High school, engineering college	Graduate courses, technical society projects, on-the-job	Work with marketing to develop products customers need	Become chief engineer, become department manager
Market research worker	High school, business administration college	Graduate courses, technical society projects	Investigate extent of markets for standard or new products, determine customers' needs	Become marketing manager, advertising manager, dealer, business methods manager
Product engineer	High school, agricultural college, engineering college	Graduate courses, technical society projects	Work in marketing department, interpret customer needs, help dealers solve customer problems, plan for market investigation	Become marketing manager, sales manager, sales representative. Buy own dealership, become manufacturer

Job	Education	Training	Duties	Opportunities
Purchasing manager	High school, technical courses	Special courses, purchasing association projects	Determine needs of factory, find best source of supply, arrange for tests, interview supplier salespeople	Become head of purchasing, manager of materials
Salesperson	High school, technical school	Manufacturers' courses, on-the-job, employers' courses	Work either for maker of machines, chemicals, supplies, or for dealer, find and handle needs of customers	Become sales manager, marketing manager, advertising manager, training specialist, study for posts in other departments, such as market research
Service representative	High school, technical school	Employer's courses, on-the-job	Work for maker of machinery, supplies, train and help dealer servicepeople, aid customers with service problems	Become service manager, salesperson, dealer
Technician	High school, technical school	Special courses, employer's courses, on-the-job	Assist engineers and scientists in almost any technical area	Study to become engineer or scientist, become senior technician

70

Careers in Natural Resources

Man has learned how to create resources by discovering ways to use what nature has provided. These resources include trees, minerals, petroleum, rocks, water, fish, air, birds, and animals.

A great many of the world's most exciting jobs are found in the forests and on our rivers and streams. The oceans provide jobs for people who seek its fish and its minerals. And the various types of mines offer dozens of different careers.

FORESTRY

Forestry is close to farming. Both involve growing things. Both have jobs for men and women with educations ranging from high school to advanced college degrees. Forestry is also related to conservation of natural resources, to lumber production, and to outdoor recreation. In fact, a great many people find work in this field because they love the out-of-doors.

In a state that has vast forests, such as Wisconsin, you would very easily discover hundreds of outdoor jobs. In Menominee County, which is an "all-Indian" county, you'd

Skilled operators drive the power machines that move big logs out of the dense forests. *Allis-Chalmers Corp.*

find the Menominee tribe running its lumber industry. In the sawmill you'd find some traditional factory jobs, including office workers, truck drivers, and managers. In the sawmill you'd find *saw operators,* helpers, mechanics.

Trees for this sawmill are cut and hauled by men who

use big cutting and lifting machinery. *Axmen* cut off tops of trees before they are chopped down. Other *lumbermen* run crawler tractors that pull logs, or skidder machines that drag logs out of the deep forests.

Driving from Menominee county into the nearby Fox

Pilots and foresty workers cooperate to carry fertilizer deep into forests to help the growth of young Christmas trees.   *Allis-Chalmers Corp.*

River valley, you would see another big operation that uses trees: papermaking.

Paper mills have many jobs. Some are like those in any manufacturing plant, but some are special. Operators must run machines that chop up wood into chips. Other men run chemical operations that soften the chips. And others run papermaking machines that are often as big as a football field. There are *paper chemists* and *technicians* in these plants, too.

Lumber firms and paper mills are both tree-users and tree farmers. They own a great deal of forest land that produces the kind of trees they need. About one-third of the nation's *foresters* work for such companies. These tree managers plan the planting, the feeding, the protection, and the harvesting of the trees.

The more technical work in forestry is done by *forestry aides*. These workers are like technicians in factories and laboratories. They record tree growth and measure water in the soil. Aides also direct fire fighting, supervise road-building and watch the water level in rivers and streams. Some forestry aides work for government conservation agencies. Some work for paper and lumber firms and some for tree nurseries, mining companies, and local parks.

A great many more forestry workers are employed by federal, state, and local government agencies. These are the men and women who keep our public forests growing. They manage the cutting of full-grown trees and prepare and operate camp grounds for the public's use. They prevent or fight forest fires. They plan and build hiking trails

Park rangers must be experts in everything from planning tours to helping motorists with car troubles.   *National Park Service*

and mark canoe trails. Related to foresters are people employed in wildlife management, such as *game protection officers* and *conservation officers*.

If you were to visit a very large federal forest, you would find many special foresters. Some supervise private lumbering firms that cut mature trees. Some supervise ranchers who pay an annual fee to permit their cattle to feed on public grassland. You might visit an outdoor laboratory where foresters are testing a new way to control disease. Or you might visit a fish hatchery that keeps the streams and lakes filled with fish. Here you also would find fish and game biologists. They keep close watch on the wildlife health and food supplies needed by fish, birds and animals.

Perhaps you might find mapmakers at work. They improve the big maps used by government, campers, lumber firms and the military. These *cartographers* often gather mapmaking information with the help of airplanes.

Wherever you find many forests, you'll find research work being done in university and private laboratories. Some work concerns disease prevention. Some finds new products for wood. Other research aids pollution control. Wood scientists sometimes called *wood technologists* do many things. Some find new ways to use wood. Some develop machinery for making things from wood.

Laboratories also need another kind of scientist: the *entomologist*. These workers study insects and their effect on natural resources, agriculture, and man. They help develop plants that resist certain insects. Entomologists also find ways to control insects.

A mapmaker—or cartographer—in the U.S. Forest Service checks over details on a new piece of work.   *U.S. Forest Service*

Today, many young people are already involved in forestry and the forests. Their schools may have tree forests or they may help every year in tree planting projects. Many adults belong to conservation clubs or camping clubs.

Many specialized workers are conservationists, as are the foresters. Together, they try to keep what we have in good condition. Related to them is the *soil conservationist*. He or she helps local governments, county agents, foresters, and private firms preserve the land. The soil conservationists show us how to prevent water runoff and how to restore forests and meadows.

FISHING

Fishing is one of the world's oldest occupations and sports combined. As a business in the United States and Canada, commercial fishing earns almost 700 million dollars a year. Thousands of people are employed in fish conservation and research. Other thousands process fish products. Vocational schools in fishing communities train young people for careers in fishing. Some *fishermen* work alone or with a helper or two on their small boats. Others have large fishing fleets with complete crews of sailors, radiomen, navigators, sonar operators, and mechanics. As you can imagine, most of the crew's work involves fish catching, sorting, and storage.

Some big fishing boats are floating factories that process fish as fast as they are caught. Some even have fish meal plants that cook and grind up fish for use in cattle, dog,

Fishermen-in-training learn how to haul nets and to keep their equipment in good condition.   *Clover Park Schools, Lakewood, Washington*

and cat food. Big fishing and processing firms have *nutritionists* and *technicians* who plan preparation methods and machinery used in the processing plants.

MINING

A lot of people are unfamiliar with mining jobs. Mining is often done far from population centers. You can see oil wells working all alone in the middle of fields. Only sand and gravel plants operate right next to the highways and out in the open.

79

This is a factory on wheels. The operators run this rolling rock-sand crushing and sifting plant in a quarry. *Allis-Chalmers Corp.*

Most of the work in these minerals production industries is done by machinery. Many of the workers have jobs that are special for their industry.

For example, in a rock quarry you would find a *crusherman* who runs huge machines that break rock. You also would meet *drillers* and *dynamiters,* who prepare rocks for blasting loose. And you would meet a *pumpman,* who runs the machines that remove water from the working area. Some work in quarries involves planning future work. Here is where *surveyors,* who measure the land,and their helpers, the *rodmen* and *chainmen,* are important. Rodmen and chainmen carry and stretch out the measuring equipment. *Shovel operators* lift the loose rock or sand.

Some of the jobs in an underground mine are also very special. In a mine you'd meet a *mine captain,* who is in charge of most mining operations at all times, and his helpers, the *shift bosses.* A *timberman* arranges for supporting timber to prevent cave-ins, and a *skip tender,* operates an elevator. There are first-class and second-class *miners,* who operate the mining machinery.

There are some very common jobs in mines and quarries, such as *carpenters, electricians, mechanics* and *repairmen,* helpers and laborers, *truck drivers, lift truck operators.* The offices have clerks and secretaries, telephone operators and janitors. There may be chemists and technicians in the laboratories, even photographers.

Mining engineers and *draftsmen* are important workers. They plan construction and guide operations.

The most important of all minerals production is petroleum and natural gas drilling, refining, and distribution. In both crude oil and gas production, everything starts with exploration. *Geologists* and *petroleum engineers* seek clues to possible oil and gas fields. They set the stage for

Mining engineers and foremen watch as the first part of a cutting machine pokes through a wall in a mine tunnel.   *American Metal Climax, Inc.*

drillers who actually pump out the natural products. Following the explorers are *pipeline builders*. Their snaking tubes carry the oil or gas to refineries.

Members of the exploration teams include *geophysicists*. They direct research and record effects of underground explosions. There are also *drillers* who run drilling machines, and *blasters,* who fire the explosives that help determine what's hidden in the earth.

If oil, for example, is suspected, petroleum engineers and drilling teams take over. A *rig builder* and his helpers put up drilling machines. A *derrickman* helps remove worn drills and keeps mud flowing down to cool the drill when it becomes hot. A *cable-tool driller* studies the rock and controls the drilling force. *Pumpers* and their helpers operate the equipment that pushes the oil away from the oil well into pipes or into storage.

People are just as involved with our natural resources today as they were thousands of years ago. But today there is a need for conservation and cleanliness. Man is learning how to renew what he has taken from nature. He plants new trees, cleans the water, and breeds new fish. Chemists and physicists are finding uses for materials that were not useful before. New materials mean new jobs. The natural resources field is opening wider every day.

Petroleum engineers watch the performance of an oil pump.

Panhandle Eastern Pipeline Co.

JOBS IN NATURAL RESOURCES

Job	Education	Training	Duties	Opportunities
Axman	High school	On-the-job	Fell trees, remove branches	Train for more complex forestry jobs
Blaster	High school	On-the-job, sometimes manufacturers' classes	Set up and detonate explosives	Become foreman, superintendent
Carpenter	High school	On-the-job, sometimes apprenticeship	Erect structures of wood used in production, maintenance, processing	Train for more complex jobs
Chainman	High school	On-the-job, technical school	Measure distances using a sort of tape line	Become surveyor, pit engineer, foreman
Chief electrician	High school, technical school	On-the-job, manufacturers' school	Direct work of electricians in repairing electrical equipment, setting up internal power lines	Become manager of maintenance, plant superintendent
Chip machine operator	High school	On-the-job	Run equipment that chews up logs into chips for papermaking	Become foreman, plant superintendent
Compressor station operator	High school	On-the-job, sometimes manufacturers' classes	Run compressor machines	Train for more advanced equipment, become foreman, chief mechanic

Job	Education	Training	Duties	Opportunities
Crusher operator	High school	On-the-job	Run machines that crush rock	Become foreman, repairman, operator of more complex equipment, maintenance manager/master mechanic, shift boss
Derrickman	High school	On-the-job	Guide pipe in and out of oil wells, work high up on a platform	Operate more complex equipment, become chief driller or chief mechanic
Driller	High school	On-the-job	Operate powered tools that punch holes in rock, ore	Become shift boss, foreman, operator of more complex equipment
Entomologist	High school, college	Government courses, graduate work	Control insects that hurt trees	Become laboratory director, research chief, work for manufacturer, teach
Fisherman	High school, technical school	On-the-job, government courses	Operate boats, nets and cleaning equipment used in fishing; prepare bait, mend equipment	Expand fleet, open processing plant, work for larger fishing firm
Fish, game biologist	High school, college	Advanced studies	Study life and growth of wildlife, health, food, disease, advise other technical workers	Advance to more complex scientific posts, become teacher, become researcher

Job	Education	Training	Duties	Advancement
Forestry aide	High school, technical school	On-the-job, employer schools	Gather information, keep records, help with experiments	Study for more advanced jobs in government service, private firms. Take college degree in forestry, similar fields
Fourdrinier operator	High school, technical school	On-the-job, paper machine makers' courses	Run entire papermaking machine	Become mill superintendent
Game protection officer	High school	On-the-job, government courses	Prevent illegal hunting, trapping, theft, trespass	Study for more advanced posts in natural resources control and management
General foreman, quarry	High school, technical school, sometimes college	On-the-job	Direct detailed work, assign foremen and their workers	Study, train for posts in general management, become equipment dealer
Mine captain	Same	Same	Same	Same
Mining engineer	College	Same	Plan construction, equipment setup, exploration	Become general executive, chief of engineering
Oiler	High school	On-the-job	Select oils to lubricate machines, add and change oil on schedule	Train for more complex maintenance work, become master mechanic, become equipment operator or shift boss

Occupation	Education	Training	Duties	Advancement
Paper chemist	High school, college	Graduate studies, employers' schools	Investigate nature of rag, wood used for paper, invent new techniques and papers	Become chief chemist, become general management executive, teach
Petroleum engineer	High school, college	Graduate study; employers' courses	Exploration, plan for drilling, do research	Advance into complex engineering assignments, become chief engineer, manager of research. Move into general management
Pumpman	High school	On-the-job	Setup and operate pumps that keep pits and shafts dry, do some maintenance	Become shift boss, study for more complex work
Quarry superintendent	High school, possibly college	On-the-job, manufacturers' schools	Direct all quarry operations	Become company executive, become equipment dealer or manufacturer, become contractor
Saw operator	High school	On-the-job	Run saw in lumber mill	Advance to foreman
Shift boss, mining	High school	On-the-job, manufacturers' schools	Foreman of men working in a single 8-hour period	Become mine captain or superintendent or assistant superintendent
Tree manager	High school, technical school	On-the-job, government courses	Direct planting, thinning, feeding operations in a planted forest	Advance to more complex management posts, become chief forester, chief of cutting operations

How Do You Make a Start?

If agribusiness fields are so numerous and so big, how do you get started?

It's easier than you think.

Your county agent's office is the best place to start. Are you curious about cattle or corn, peaches or pigs, Christmas trees or cantaloupe? Or tractors? Or vocational courses and agricultural colleges? The county agent, or your school guidance counselor, can direct you to a great many associations, government agencies, or schools that will send you envelopes of material.

Every state has a land-grant college that offers four-year courses in natural resource subjects suitable to the state. There are also special colleges, such as schools of mines. Colleges like these also offer a great many short courses for beginners and skilled workers alike. In addition, a great many communities have technical vocational schools that concentrate on job training suitable to the community. Schools in cattle states concentrate on livestock, for example.

A very important source of information is the U.S. Labor Department's *Occupational Outlook Handbook,* (U.S.

This student is studying the effect of plant foods. Perhaps it will lead her to a career in natural resources. *University of Alaska*

Printing Office, Washington, D.C. 20402) issued every other year. After each occupational chapter there is a list of names and addresses of important other sources of job information. Some of these are government agencies, some are industrial associations. There are hundreds of special associations that list jobs requiring some special skill. The labor department lists some of these special jobs and a great many of the typical jobs found anywhere.

And there are other things to do:

1. Investigate every community you can reach near your home. Using the phone book, make up a list of all the agribusiness firms. Ask the county agent's advice, too. Visit or write these firms. Learn what beginning jobs are available.

Sometimes getting into a career starts with a program sponsored by a manufacturer. These young men took part in a building design project.
Armco Steel Corp.

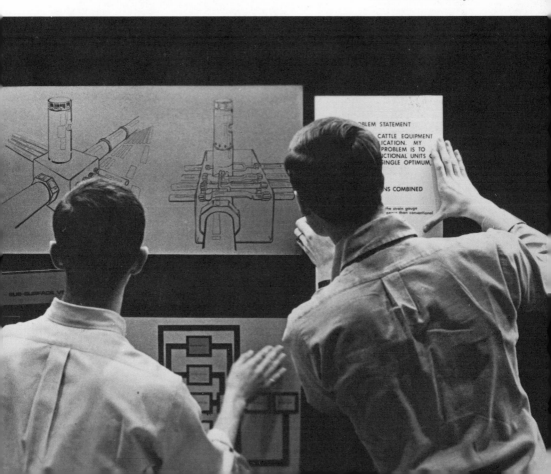

Jobs in Agribusiness

2. Identify all the production farming, horticultural, forestry, conservation, and animal-bird raising operations near you. Find out what jobs are open to beginners and what simple courses are available. Check on seasonal work.

3. If you belong to a young people's group develop a program involving talks by people from the natural resources business.

4. Visit plants that process foods, metals, oil, gas, or make machinery. Find out what their relationship is to agribusiness and natural resources. Find out what the entry jobs consist of and what training is needed.

5. Find and visit federal and state parks and forests. See what part-time or entry jobs are available.

Index to Careers

Index to Career Photos

630.23
HOU   Houlehen, Robert J.

              Jobs in agribusi-
              ness

DATE DUE			
FEB 28			
FEB 28			
APR 26 '83			
APR 15			